The Storm Left No Flowers

poems by

Barbara Robidoux

Finishing Line Press
Georgetown, Kentucky

The Storm Left No Flowers

Copyright © 2018 by Barbara Robidoux
ISBN 978-1-63534-797-5 First Edition
All rights reserved under International and Pan-American Copyright Conventions. No part of this book may be reproduced in any manner whatsoever without written permission from the publisher, except in the case of brief quotations embodied in critical articles and reviews.

ACKNOWLEDGMENTS

Grateful acknowledgement is made to the following publications, where versions of these poems have appeared:

In Medias Res: "Antelope"
Off the Coast: "Ode to Acadia"

Publisher: Leah Maines
Editor: Christen Kincaid
Cover Art: Teresa Candelaria
Author Photo: Teresa Candelaria
Cover Design: Leah Huete

Printed in the USA on acid-free paper.
Order online: www.finishinglinepress.com
        also available on amazon.com

        Author inquiries and mail orders:
            Finishing Line Press
             P. O. Box 1626
        Georgetown, Kentucky 40324
               U. S. A.

Table of Contents

Preface xi

The World As We Knew It Is Broken 1

Ode to Acadia 2

Out of Ashes 3

Wild Fire 5

Antelope 6

Abiquiu 9

Kasha Katuwe 12

Flood 13

The Petrogluphs of La Cieneguilla 14

The Storm Left No Flowers 15

Los Aguajes 16

Notes 17

These poems are dedicated to all the children who will inherit this earth and to my grandson Isaiah Mailhot

PREFACE

We live in the midst of the sixth mass extinction on our planet and experience very significant global climate changes. It is a confusing time for some. Fire and water rage. Murderous storms kill thousands. With every massive earthquake the earth changes the tilt on her axis. Traditional Inupiat hunters tell us the sun rises and sets in a changed location. They are unable to carry out their hunts as usual.

The world as we knew it is broken.

Despite the destruction leveled by natural disasters, the earth maintains her beauty. These poems pay homage to a home place where I landed more than twenty years ago. I came from the shores of the north Atlantic where I was born and lived into middle age. The high desert of northern New Mexico has now become my home. The elements of earth, wind, fire and water all contribute to an ever shifting landscape that displays tremendous beauty in these change times.

Barbara Robidoux
Santa Fe, New Mexico
2018

THE WORLD AS WE KNEW IT IS BROKEN

Their waters now unlivable, pilot whales beach themselves
in great numbers along the eastern shores—
they will return to live on the land
as they did in the old times.

Winter never came to New England,
we had to suck the sap
from maple trees
with vacuums.

A polar bears dies from lack of ice,
then lack of food.
Glaciers shrink, ocean waters warm.
We have melted the poles of the planet.

In winter off Nantucket Island
bottle-nosed dolphins circle the harbor
instead of swimming the deep waters to migrate south.
An old woman stands on the shore
and watches, then tells no one:

"They have come for me."
Without looking back,
she walks into the frigid water.

In the mountains pines and aspens
are heaving great sighs.
I walk and listen to tall trees.
My sparrow fingers collect their seeds
in case they too will
move away.

ODE TO ACADIA

Here, the dead are not buried, they dissolve

                 into the mists, bones upon bones
shift in the night.

Yellow eyes of snowy owls

                         on a flight south, stop

near the fast rising waters of Acadia.

Furious winds rearrange my life,

                         your voyage across my breasts

reminds me to breathe.

In the dawn hours
                 of sit and wait,

yellow eyes search for food.

Traplines follow the river

                         an intricate web cast for fur.

Muskrats, minks and martens stolen.

My hands frozen, I cannot protest.

My pulse slows to a murmur

In Acadia all breaths are numbered,

preserved in ice, they settle into the land.

OUT OF ASHES

Tonight the crescent moon holds water,
refuses to release rain on this dry town.
The old ones tell stories
in time the earth will dry,
fires will transform the land.
Out of ashes we will live again.

It is the sound of apricot buds bursting,
of snows melting on the Sangres
of new leaves unfurling,
that diminishes the fear of police
sirens screaming in the night.

In a dry field behind the house
a tiny leopard frog lives buried in the red earth.
She patiently waits for spring rains
to release her to the land.
A pair of golden eagles fly overhead,
they hunt rabbits and prairie dogs.
Red tailed hawks eye chickens in the yard.
This is not a country place.
It is a south side barrio of dark skinned people.
Trailer homes sprout up in a land
too dry for their survival.
Moonlight shines on junkies
who patrol dry arroyos.

Stories are told by Aztec dancers.
At the end of a fifty-two year cycle
they lit a fire,
danced around it and blessed themselves.
Bare feet, arms and legs passed through the flames
hair burning.
They drank chocolate mixed with chili,
Told stories of a time when the eagle and condor
will meet again.

A circle of grandmothers
meet on Sunday afternoons
in an old tin-roofed adobe.
We eat oranges, drink strong tea
step outside in the March wind.
Dust in our faces, tumble weeds
throw themselves against our legs
while we pray for rain.

We beg the ancestors to bring back
the water honoring songs.

Fires devour forest of ponderosa pine.
Bosques go up in flames.
Salt cedar fuels the path
to ancient cottonwoods
singing their death song.

A desert sun rises above the naked Sangres.

WILD FIRE

Each night a blood red burning sun
descends into plumes of smoke.
Four months without rain.
Fire has taken hold of this land.
One hundred forty thousand acres burned
so hot in places the earth's skin has melted.
Igneous rock turned to magma.

At Santa Clara Indians walk
the dusty pueblo roads.
Ghosts, they look for their ancestors.
Sacred sites have burned,
prayer feathers turned to ashes.
A once pristine watershed is destroyed.
Lakes filled with silt, river turned black with ash.
The fire continues north and west
diverted from a nuclear site towards the pueblo.
Deer and elk run until their hearts burst.
The wind becomes one with the fire.

Black mesa is shrouded in smoke.
I carry beans, chili, green salad,
turn left at the last cattle guard.
A pueblo mourns.

ANTELOPE

> *The antelope are strange people… They are beautiful to look at, and yet they are tricky. We do not trust them. They appear and disappear; they are like shadows on the plains. Because of their great beauty, young men sometimes follow antelope and are lost forever. Even if those foolish ones find themselves and return, they are never right again in their heads.*
>
> *Pretty Shield Medicine Woman of the Crows*

At dusk along highway 16
towards the pueblo of Cochiti
a small herd of antelope
grazes in the flatlands
beside the road.

They have come down from the mountains
as if to allow us to see them
so we can know their wildness,
so we might remember
the miracle of fresh grass
in a desert field
after a winter of good snow.

Darkness descends.
The herd vanishes.
I try to follow them
but they are too fast.

In the village cedar and pinon smoke rises then settles in the old
    cottonwoods.
An old woman, her hair hangs braided to her waist, invites me to
    visit in her small adobe home.
We sit by her fire and talk. Her face is cut deep with wrinkles and
    her dark eyes shine.
She smiles when she hears the antelope have returned.

"I have something," she tells me. "A recipe for antelope stew. This is medicine. Even when we butcher them, there is a sweetness that comes out of them and fills the air."

ABIQUIU
Screech of an Owl

I.

A tiny cabin sits by a meandering river. I am inside. A rocking chair and army cot, my friends. I wash in an old porcelain wash bowl, brush my teeth outside the door. A large window faces the Rio Chama and north facing windows near the ceiling provide light. It is a one room pine built cabin with a door to the south and another to the west. Sunsets are beyond words here.

At night beaver come ashore to feed. They sharpen their teeth on young cottonwoods, river willows and a hedge of privet that surrounds the cabin. They slap their tails on this fertile earth, slide in and out of a lodge they have built in the middle of the river.

By day silence except for bird songs. I breathe in quiet. My city living soul nourished. *"This is an ancient place"* the 200 year old cottonwoods whisper. Like old women gossiping they lean together and watch over what was once floodplain. A dam was built at Abiquiu. The old village of Genizaros flooded by humans who thought they could control the water of Rio Chama. What fools to think water could be held, then set free on their whims.

There are cycles here. I have come to listen, to look and to fall into the rhythms of this place. It is early spring. Beaver kits are being born as I write this. Roots of river grasses and willows stir, awaken to new growth.

> the strength
> of trout lilies and black flies
> purple iris on my path

II.

And I lay down in the tall grasses flattened by beavers. They rested here and now I rest and watch this meandering Rio Chama make its way to the Rio Grande.

The river knows me by my breath. It slows me, settles me into sleep. Water dreams.

I wake. Step over a barbed wire fence, push aside willows and cattails until I reach the shore. I bend to touch water. It has lost its chill midday. Overhead a great blue heron flies to the other side of a beaver lodge, stops to fish.

The elders say the water and land remember us. We leave our breath, our sweat wherever we walk. Memory lives in the place.

> ancient cottonwoods
> and the black bear
> remember our laughter

III.

Spring comes in with fierce wind. Dust in your face and the threat that peach and apple blossoms will freeze. Winter has always been my friend. The long nights to dream. Snow to walk on, I know what to expect, Spring is unpredictable, has a mind of its own.

In the distance the Pedernal watches. The outside world is tattered, torn to its core. Here I can feel my breath.

> along Rio Chama
> a murder of crows
> gossip in cottonwoods

IV.

In Plaza Blanca the old genizaro recovers from another stroke. His red headband shifts to one side to match the new twist of his face. Down the hill from his house the door of San Tomas Apostol church is wide open. I enter and light a candle for myself. Holy water in the font is cool on my forehead I make the sign of the cross and leave. Across the plaza, Rosa Trujillo has not opened the door of the tiny library. Our gossip will have to wait for another time.

An old man with a wide smile and very big ears drives an old dented Chevy Nova and stops beside me. He wants to know how he can transport and even older man who sits beside him on the torn car seat to a friend's house. The friend lives at the end of an overgrown foot path from the plaza. "No sé, burro or wheelbarrow," I reply with a chuckle.

Life moves slowly in old Abiquiu Pueblo. Autumn relinquishes its hold and makes way for winter. Snow on the Sangres even before Dia de los Muertos.

> an old adobe home
> broken walls, empty windows
> returns to the earth

V.

Pedernal, flat topped mesa of flaking stone sits blue against red hills. We wait for Changing Woman to be born again into a slate gray sky. Snows from Colorado push their way into the valley of Abiquiu. Sandhill cranes have moved north leaving eagles and ravens to speak the old language. They etch it into the land of pinon and juniper, let it float on the water of Rio Chama. Not to be forgotten.

> stories told with petroglyphs
> remind us
> there was a time before today.

VI.

Early November. The dead remembered, cottonwoods scream yellow as the veils are closing. I step into the silence, as necessary to me as a warm bath.

Fallen leaves carpet the path to the cabin and beyond. I gather up the quiet as though to bundle it and take it back to the city. Yellow leaves, the damp scent of the river.

The river keeps everything moving. Sometimes at a furious pace. Angry. But today Rio Chama moves slowly, peacefully.

A new beaver dam sticks its jagged head out of the water in front of the cabin. Beavers appear at dawn and dusk. These flat tailed creatures mate for life.

> cold autumn night
> river willows redden
> while I sleep

VII.

The old genizaro died in his sleep, in his bed, in his home, in Abiquiu Plaza where he had lived all of his 85 years.

They buried him in the plaza near the old ruined church. No one had dug in that earth for many years but it received him like he was an old friend.

> in the bottomless night
> before rain came down
> the screech of an owl

KASHA KATUWE

The winds of Kasha Katuwe
hurl sand in my eyes,
my ears, my nose

a ponderosa pine tree bends
holds tight to spiraled rocks
distressed roots grow deeper

blue, blue sky
half moon leans toward earth
promise of rain in a dry year

thousand year old lichens
cling to igneous rocks
remember a time
when water ruled here

in the shallow arroyo
I cross tracks of jack rabbits and deer
my own treaded foot prints
settle into this place

above Kasha Katuwe watch
a cholla cactus lies down
fainted by wind and drought
caught in its withered roots
candy wrappers and cigarette butts
relics of our time

ponderosas felled by wildfires
pinon and one seed junipers
devoured by bark beetles
migrating geese thrown off course
by earth's new tilt

the wind, the wind
our ferocious faith keeper
scribe of ghosts.

FLOOD

The sky opened so we could remember the sounds of rushing water.

Rivers overturned banks and pushed into the bosques: The Santa Fe, the Chama, the Rio Grande, the Pecos.

After months of drought we heard rain night and day. We forgot the sun.

Footprints of summer were erased by the rain.

In the canyon villages people ran for higher ground. Water rushed off the mountains, destroying everything in its path. In a desert land that had thirsted for years, we knew water to be the great healer. Now epic floods devoured great slabs of the earth. In the mountains whole villages were swept away. Roads disappeared and water reshaped the land. Animals fled, left behind their homelands inundated by a one hundred year flood.

> torrential rain
> canyonlands turned to rivers
> a velvet queen sunflower
> searches
> for the sun.

THE PETROGLYPHS OF LA CIENEGUILLA

The trail is muddy from recent rains. Scent of juniper heavy in the air. It is a gray cloudy day cold but warm for January in Santa Fe. In two days Donald J. Trump will be inaugurated as the 45th president of the United States. It is a troubling time.

I have come to the petroglyphs of La Cieneguilla for the solace and quiet of these ancient rock paintings. The petroglyphs are protected by the state of New Mexico. They are on BLM land that is designated an area of "critical concern". Strands of barbed wire are loosely strung along a path that runs along the bottom of the cliffs. All along this fence there are breaks in the wire inviting humans to enter and explore. I enter a break and approach the rocks that have fallen from the cliffs. With the rains it is too dangerous to climb today.

This is a quiet place. No others are here this cold January day. Cane cholla bones are strewn among the rocks. Coyote scat reveals the fur of a rabbit.

I stop to look closely at a rock that has fallen from the cliff. Its insides are revealed. Muted shades of orange, blue, gray even silver. The rock vibrates in an unusual way even though it has settled into the red earth for some time, surrounded by weeds and grasses. Its voice is of another time. It consoles me, reminds me to remember the sanctity and continuum of life on this planet.

> out of rocks
> painted with stories
> star people walk into my life

THE STORM LEFT NO FLOWERS

The earth shakes. How many times can I say I love you?

I pull on a pair of wool socks, slide under the covers.

Cat gently pushes into my thigh.

TV News reports massive earthquake in Mexico, Popo erupts.

Remnants of an ancient Aztec temple Ehecatl rise up.

under a shopping mall in Mexico city.   Popo erupts.

The curandera tells me the earth's umbilical cord

is going back to the moon.

"Align yourself with the good winds."

Puerto Rico O! Puerto Rico,

Maria has ravaged you.

Three million without food and water.   Powerless.

A dead cow hangs from the top of a broken telephone pole,

placed there by the winds.

Bees are dying. They have no food.

The storm left no flowers.

I tell you for the thousandth time "I love you."

This is not the end, not yet.

LOS AGUAJES

I walk an ancient pueblo
                abandoned by ancestors

who dried corn on their roofs
                walked a crocked path

to fetch water from a river,
                etched messages on smooth canyon walls.

Today blue agaves
                grow out of river rocks.

Nopales turn red in the January sun.
                A circle of pottery shards reveal

a shrine to those who left

                this land to drought.

Seven hundred years later
                          it is the same red earth

who cries for water.

We have forgotten the songs to call down the clouds.

Our feet no longer remember dances for rain.

Drought is a faceless monster

who hides

under

the skin of this high desert.

NOTES

p.11 Genizaro—a person of mixed ancestry. plains Indian and perhaps Hopi, Pueblo and Spanish

p.14 "Kasha Katuwe"—also known as tent rocks on the Cochiti Pueblo.

p.17 Ehecatl—god of wind

p.18 Los Aguajes—a thirteen century pueblo whose ruins lie 15 miles south west of Santa Fe, New Mexico

Barbara Robidoux is the author of the poetry collection *Migrant Moon* (Miriam's Well 2012). Her poetry has appeared in journals and anthologies nationwide including *In Medias Res* and *Off the Coast. Bearing the Mask; Southwestern Persona Poems, Hinchas de Poesia.*

Barbara also writes fiction, which has appeared in the *Denver Quarterly,* the *Yellow Medicine Review,* the *Santa Fe Literary Review, Dawnland Voices*, and numerous anthologies. *Sweetgrass Burning: Stories from the Rez*, a collection of linked short stories, was released by Blue Hand Books in February 2016. The novella *The Legacy of Lucy Little Bear* was released by Blue Hand Books in March 2017.

Barbara holds an MFA from the Institute of American Indian Arts, an MA from Vermont College, and a BA from the University of New Hampshire. She lives in Santa Fe, New Mexico, where she is at work on a forthcoming novel and works as faculty at the Institute of American Indian Arts MFA program in creative writing.